A knockout show

Story written by Adrian Bradbury
Illustrated by Tim Archbold

Speed Sounds

Consonants

Ask your child to say the sounds (not the letter names) clearly and quickly, in and out of order. Make sure he or she does not add 'uh' to the end of the sounds, e.g. 'f' not 'fuh'.

Each box contains one sound. Focus sounds for this story are circled.

f	l	m	n	r	s	v	z	sh	th	ng
ff	ll	mm	nn	rr	ss	ve	zz			nk
ph	le	mb	kn	wr	se		**se**			
			gn		**c**		s			
					ce					

b	c	d	g	h	j	p	qu	t	w	x	y	ch
bb	k	dd	gg		g	pp		tt	wh			tch
	ck		gu		ge							
					dge							

Vowels

Ask your child to say the sounds in and out of order.

a	e ea	i	o	u	ay	ee y	igh i	ow o
at	h**e**n	**i**n	**o**n	**u**p	d**ay**	s**ee**	h**igh**	bl**ow**

oo	oo	ar	or oor ore	air	ir	ou	oy oi
z**oo**	l**oo**k	c**ar**	f**or**	f**air**	wh**ir**l	sh**ou**t	b**oy**

Story Green Words

For each word ask your child to read the separate sounds, e.g. 'b-u-s', 'p-oo-l' and then blend sounds together to make the word, e.g. 'bus', 'pool'. Sometimes one sound is represented by more than one letter, e.g. 'th', 'oo'. These are underlined.

Troy coins round voice noise

Ask your child to say the syllables and then read the whole word.

knock|out splen|did bat|ons fan|tas|tic tap-|danc|ing

brill|i|ant rea|lly

Ask your child to read the root first and then the whole word with the suffix.

agree → agreed judge → judges bellow → bellowed

juggle → juggling shout → shouting loud → loudly

sulk → sulked drop → dropped disappoint → disappointed

Vocabulary Check

Tell your child the meaning of each word in the context of the story.

	definition:	**sentence:**
splendid	*wonderful*	*The judges... joined the acts for a splendid show.*
batons	*special clubs for juggling*	*She juggled with batons...*
tumbling	*gymnastics*	*He did an incredible tumbling display.*
bellowed	*shouted very loudly*	*"What a knockout act!" bellowed Troy.*
stomped	*walked angrily*	*Taylor stomped away... and tripped and fell over his feet.*

Red Words

Red words don't sound like they look. Ask your child to read the words but if he or she gets stuck read the word to your child.

anyone	two	your	to
once	son	who	other
was	would	water	could
over	all	does	through
ball	said	my	there

A knockout show

Do not read the story to your child first. Point to the words as your child reads. If your child gets stuck on a word help him or her say the sounds and blend them together. Re-read each sentence to your child to help him or her remember what he or she has read. Discuss what is happening on each page.

It was the last round of *Knockout Talent*. The judges – Holly, Marta and Troy – joined the acts for a splendid show.

The show kicked off with Juggling Jin.

Juggling Jin juggled with ping pong balls… and dropped them. She juggled with batons and then with coins… and dropped them too.

"Hmm," began judge Marta. "I was a bit disappointed with that. When you juggle, it's best if you catch the things you throw!"

Next up was Sammy 'The Star' Smith. He sang – very loudly!

"For a little boy, you have a *big* voice," said judge Holly. "Sadly, I found it a bit too loud. What a noise!"

Tip Tap Taylor was next, with his tap-dancing act that didn't go to plan.

"You have very fast feet," admitted judge Troy, "but I didn't really enjoy your act. It spoiled it for me when you tripped up and fell flat on your back."

The next act was Molly and Dolly. Dolly was a dog who did tricks – but she didn't want to do her tricks very well today.

"That wasn't brilliant," said Marta to Molly. "When you pointed to the left, Dolly ran to the right. When you pointed at the cuddly toy, Dolly went for my boot."

Last up was Bendy Bob. He did an incredible tumbling display.

“Fantastic!” shouted Holly.
“What a knockout act!” bellowed Troy.
“You really are a star of tomorrow!” screeched Marta.

They all agreed –
Bendy Bob was the top act!

Jin was second, and got a big box of chocs... which she dropped.
Sammy sobbed... very noisily.
Taylor stomped away... and tripped and fell over his feet.
Molly sulked off, shouting for Dolly to follow... but Dolly just lay there and destroyed Marta's boot.

Now ask your child to re-read the story helping him or her think about the best way to read each sentence.

Questions to talk about

Read the questions aloud to your child and ask him or her to find the answers on the relevant pages. Do not ask your child to read the questions – the words are harder than he or she can read at the moment.

p.9 What were the three judges called?

p.10 Why was Marta disappointed with Juggling Jin's act?

p.11 Why does Sammy call himself 'The Star'?

p.12 What spoiled Tip Tap Taylor's act?

p.13 Why didn't Molly and Dolly's act go as planned?

p.14 Why did the judges think Bendy Bob was the best act?

p.15 Who do you think was the worst act? Why?

Questions to read and answer

Ask your child to read the questions and find the correct answer in the story.

1. Juggling Jin juggled with **ping pong balls / footballs / tennis balls**.

2. Sammy's singing was **good / loud / boring**.

3. Tip Tap Taylor's act was **tap-dancing / tumbling / singing**.

4. When Molly pointed to the left, Dolly **ran to the left / picked up the cuddly toy / ran to the right**.

5. **Sammy 'The Star' Smith / Bendy Bob / Juggling Jin** was given a box of chocs.

Speedy Green Words

Ask your child to read the words clearly and quickly – across the rows, down the columns, and in and out of order.

boy	feet	toy	too
throw	enjoy	away	found
loud	shouted	lay	next
right	show	boot	for
boy	loud	sang	round